To our parents,
Anne Davidson Ferry
and David Russell Ferry.

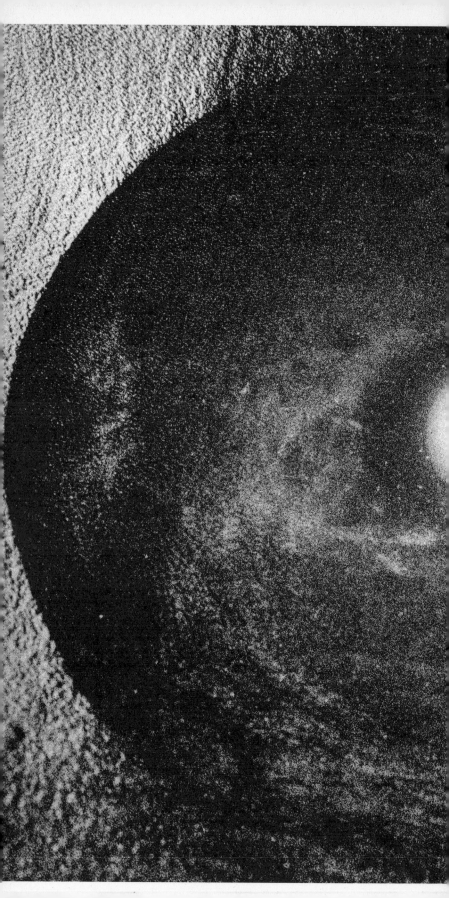

CONTENTS
========

INTRODUCTION
==============

La Batea looks closely at small-scale gold mining in
Colombia, work that is often ignored or stigmatized in
public debates and official discourse. We also document
the struggles of gold mining communities to resist
destruction at the hands of both criminal organizations
and multinational corporations. In many places, these
communities resist even in the face of death threats and
armed attacks.

For better and for worse, gold has been central to
Colombia's history. Pre-Columbian cultures, such as the
Tayrona, Muisca, Quimbaya and Tierradentro, developed
advanced technologies and aesthetic practices with gold,
which was fundamental to their ritual and political life. When
the Spaniards arrived in these lands, they brought their
own beliefs about gold as a profoundly powerful economic,
political, and metaphysical substance.

Europeans' search for gold in the Americas crystallized
in the legend of a city of gold, known as El Dorado (in
Spanish, "The Golden One"). This famous myth arose from
a misunderstanding: the Spaniards sought a golden city,
but really the term referred to a Muisca ritual held on Lake
Guatavita, north of what is now Bogotá. In this ceremony, as
recounted in 1636 by the colonial chronicler Juan Rodríguez
Freyle, the heir to the chief was covered in gold powder and
transported by boat into the middle of the lake where he threw
in offerings of gold, emeralds, and feathers. Rodríguez Freyle

concluded his description by saying "From this ceremony was taken the celebrated name of 'Dorado,' which has cost so many lives." In search of El Dorado, the *conquistadores* plundered countless native cities, villages, and graves.

Throughout the 16th century, indigenous populations collapsed because of disease, forced labor under brutal conditions, and warfare with the Spanish. To replace their labor, the Spanish introduced thousands of Africans as slaves, especially to mine gold in the Pacific and Antioquia regions. Many escaped and formed maroon communities that supported themselves through mining, along with fishing, hunting, and agriculture. Others who remained enslaved also engaged in these economic practices to feed their families.

To finance the War of Independence, Simón Bolívar leased major gold mines, such as those in Marmato, to British concerns. In the republican period, steam technology and later, railroads, helped to establish underground mining as a major source of Colombian wealth. For most of the 19th century Colombia was the world's largest producer of gold.

By the late 20th century, Colombia's internal war and particularly the high risk of kidnapping and extortion by leftist guerrillas made foreign gold companies reluctant to do business in Colombia. However, beginning in the early 2000s, a combination of high metals prices, more efficient technologies, and improved security conditions made Colombia attractive for transnational corporations.

The Colombian government prioritizes large-scale resource extraction as a central feature of its economic development agenda. The current mining code was drafted in 2001 in collaboration with Canadian advisers, and favors large-scale projects. Foreign mining companies now see Colombia as a new resource frontier.

In all this excitement, the government and foreign corporations tend to ignore local communities that have been mining gold for centuries. At least 350,000 Colombians make their livelihood directly through small-scale gold mining activities, with many more depending on them through family ties and commerce. These miners have dense social and territorial relations with gold, customary rights, and long histories.

As the "mining locomotive" (to use President Juan Manuel Santos's phrase) gained momentum, these local miners have come into conflict with multinational corporations and with the Colombian state. Between 2005 and 2011, the state, which owns the subsoil, issued over 9,000 mining titles for exploration and production, with nearly 1,000 for precious metal mining. For the most part, these licenses were issued without informing or consulting with miners already working in these areas, nor with agricultural, indigenous, and Afro-Colombian communities who often oppose large-scale mining in their territories. This has led to many confrontations.

At the same time, the rise in gold prices led Colombia's insurgent armies, the Revolutionary Armed Forces of Colombia (FARC) and the National Liberation Army (ELN), right-wing paramilitary militias and criminal gangs to get involved in gold mining, causing tremendous violence in many areas of the country.

As a brother-and-sister team, we come to this project from the fields of non-fiction photography and cultural anthropology. We began researching the book and making trips to different mining localities in 2011, when the gold market was at its height and conflicts surrounding mining were raging. At that time, Stephen was photographing the increasing role of gold mining in Colombia's internal armed conflict and the environmental consequences of this gold rush.

He covered important efforts by the government to combat criminal involvement in gold mining. However, it became increasingly clear that state mining agencies and national media tend to portray all small-scale miners as dangerous agents, applying the terms "illegal" and "criminal" indiscriminately. This language can then be used to justify violent displacements of people and communities that resist large mining operations.

At the same time, arguments by large mining companies, frequently repeated in the media, give the impression that small-scale miners are environmentally irresponsible holdovers of an economic practice that must inevitably give way to modernity. In place of these reductive stories, we saw a need to document multiple mining histories, practices, and experiences.

We take the *batea* —a wooden pan used in mining since Pre-Columbian times— as the emblem and title for this work. The principal implement in artisanal gold mining, the batea is a unifying practice of the miners depicted here. Historically, the batea can be understood as a symbol of freedom, being the tool used by thousands of people to buy their liberty before the abolition of slavery in the mid-19th century. Its use depends on a close encounter with rock, mud, water, and gold. The batea represents the autonomy and craft of the artisanal miner.

In the book's design, we refer to the physical experience of gold work. The materials used engage the sense of touch as well as sight. The cardboard cover is stamped with a circle of 22 karat gold leaf of the kind used by restorers of religious art in Colombia. By this, we seek to represent the way gold in a batea emerges from an earthy medium, shining forth in contrast to its rough origins.

The black and white photographs here were taken with Kodak T-Max 3200 to take advantage of the graininess of that film. Grain is made up of silver particles in the emulsion that make film sensitive to light. So the physical existence of this book depends on the mining of precious metals.

The topic of mining in Colombia is very broad and we do not pretend to give a comprehensive account of the many questions and scenarios involved. To understand the history and context for what we have seen and heard, we rely on the works of various scholars, researchers, and journalists. We do not directly cite these sources within the text. However, you can find a selected list at the end of the book.

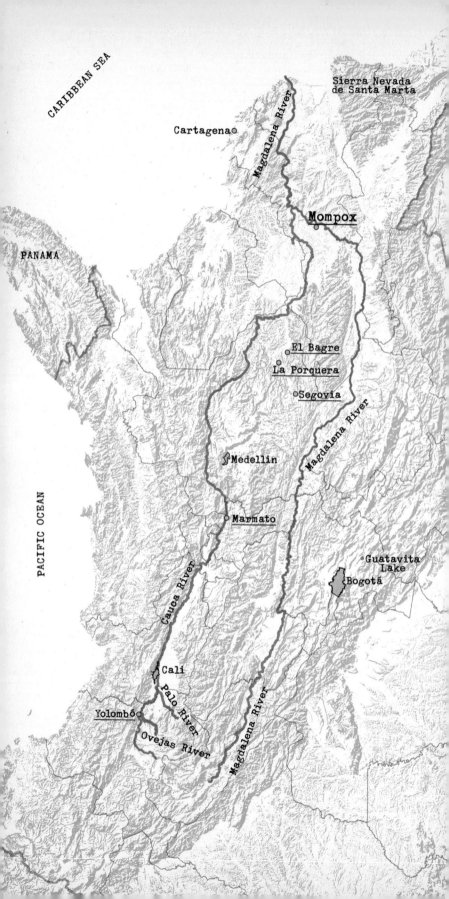

CARIBBEAN SEA

Sierra Nevada
de Santa Marta

Cartagena

PANAMA

Mompox

El Bagre

La Porquera

Segovia

Magdalena River

Medellin

PACIFIC OCEAN

Marmato

Guatavita
Lake

Bogotá

Cauca River

Cali

Palo River

Yolombó

Ovejas River

Magdalena River

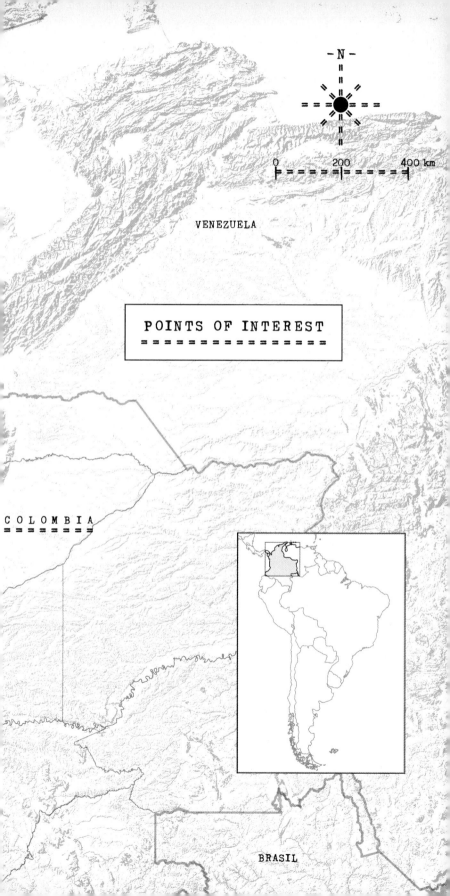

-N-

0   200   400 km

VENEZUELA

POINTS OF INTEREST
=================

COLOMBIA
========

BRASIL

PATRIMONY
=========

A sign in the Gold Museum in Bogotá, seen in January 2013, reads "Patrimony cannot be bought, nor can it be sold." However, as with most museums, the existence of the Gold Museum depends on a contradiction between that statement and its own history. Much of its vast collection was obtained by purchases of objects gotten through the looting of tombs and sacred sites, known as *guaquería*, which is widely practiced throughout South America.

This uncomfortable history is no reflection on the administrators and curators of the museum, which has professional standards for determining provenance. As they point out, had the museum not made these purchases, these gold pieces would either have been melted down, or would have been trafficked to private and public collections abroad. Indeed, before the Banco de la República began purchasing them, most Pre-Columbian gold objects did leave the country. In 1892, the Colombian government even gave over 120 gold pieces to the Queen of Spain in thanks for help settling a border dispute with Venezuela.

As the Bank's collection grew, so did an understanding of the value of these gold objects, not only for their monetary value but for their distinctive historical, cultural, and artistic significance and their importance for the nation. Today in Colombia, archaeological pieces are designated as national patrimony. In addition to being legally the property of all Colombians, they are also understood by some to be the inalienable possessions of indigenous peoples whose ancestors lived in the territories that became Colombia, and who continue to live simultaneously as Colombians and members of their own distinct communities.

However, many indigenous people do not see these objects as property, and to think of them that way could even be said to commit a kind of violence against them. In May 2008, representatives of the Kogi, Wiwa and Arhuaco people from the Sierra Nevada of Santa Marta visited the Gold Museum, accompanied by the Kogi spiritual authority (or *mama*) Shibulata Zalabata and an indigenous documentary team. These three ethnicities descend from the Tairona culture, whose sacred objects form a large part of the collection. Mama Shibulata stood in front of the human-like figures suspended behind the glass, and said that they were "in prison, they're not getting fed, not receiving visits, they shouldn't be there. Just suffering like they're being punished."

The haunting objects in the museum tell of the dispossession of indigenous Americans by Europeans over half a millennium. Though you could say the same thing about all Pre-Columbian artifacts, the fact that these are gold—doubly precious and doubly sacred—at once shows the brilliance of Pre-Columbian cultures and the scale of their dispossession.

Delegation of Kogi, Wiwa and Arhuaco indigenous
authorities in the Gold Museum. Bogotá, 2008.

Ceremonial mask, Tierradentro culture, Northeastern
Cauca region. Middle period. (150 ACE – 900 CE). Gold
Museum, Bogotá, 2016.

19

SLOW GOLD
=========

The Palo River flows down from the highlands of Santo
Domingo in the Cordillera Central mountain chain of
Colombia. Those mountains are rich in gold loposits.
The alluvial gold found in the Palo River is the result, over
millions of years, of erosion and runoff from the mountains
upstream.

Many rivers in Colombia contain such deposits. Since the
1980s, miners have used backhoes to extract gold from many
river banks and dredges to get out the ore lying within the river
beds. They use mercury to process the gold on site; the runoff
goes into the river or the surrounding soil. Such methods allow
these miners and their financial backers (a Caterpillar backhoe
costs as much as 300,000 US dollars) to quickly take out the
gold from these rivers, but they cause great damage to riverine
ecosystems.

But not all alluvial miners use such methods. Especially in
the Pacific region, where the Palo River is found, many Afro-
Colombian and indigenous miners use only wooden sluices and
bateas to extract and refine their gold. In place of mercury,
some work with the sap of a plant known popularly as *escoba
babosa* (*Sida rhombifolia*), used in South America as a remedy
for inflammation. These practices take much longer but leave
no toxic waste in the river.

One could think of these methods as "slow gold," in
reference to the Slow Food International movement. Slow
Food International seeks to transform capital - and chemical-

intensive production in favor of food produced in ways that are sustainable for the environment and fair to farmers.

In 2014, Stephen met a family from the Nasa indigenous community of Huellas, Caloto, panning for gold a few yards from their house on the Palo River. When asked if they use mercury, the father replied,

> "that stuff sickens us, and we don't want to contaminate ourselves with anything, any sickness.... We throw nothing into the river, not even plastic bags. You can bathe all day in it if you want, you will not get sick. Why? Because the river comes down from the mountain, and it is clean. And we do not dirty the water, we take care of what we have, our river, the plants, the trees, we take care of all of it."

Since then, the waters of the Palo River have become muddied. According to indigenous authorities, outsiders working with several families from the community have begun mining with backhoes:

> ...these few families are not [only] contaminated with chemical elements they use to extract gold, but they are also brainwashed to ...mine and work against the indigenous government.

In the Pacific region, many communities have mobilized the Indigenous Guard, a native police force, to remove the backhoes through dialogue or, if necessary, by force.

Batea. Río Palo, Huellas indigenous reserve. Caloto,
Cauca, 2011.

Mining sluice, Palo River, 2011.

Palo River, 20II.

Gold in batea. Palo river, 20II. -->

THE BACKHOES
============

We rode motorcycles to the village of La Porquera along
an unpaved road that wound into the hills above Zaragoza,
affording a pleasant view of its gold-painted houses. Along
the way, our guide explained that though we did have
permission to visit a mine and take photographs, we were
not, under any circumstances, to ask who controlled the
operation.

At the site, a half-dozen grim-looking men stood around
the lip of a deep crater dug out by two giant backhoes poised
on earthen platforms halfway down the hole. Seen from
below the men cut dark silhouettes against the sky, abstract
messages of menace. The walls of the man-made canyon
were etched with the marks of the backhoes, as though a
trapped dinosaur had tried to claw its way out. In the mud at
the bottom of the pit, some hundred miners were working in
a moving mass, elbow to elbow, each one loading earth into
his or her batea and then carrying it off to the side to add
mercury and separate out some particles of gold.

Every few minutes, the giant yellow machines would
emit a puff of smoke and then scrape out buckets of muck
from the hole, dropping the contents on top of several metal
ramps that stood alongside the crater. The miners at the
bottom would scramble to get a footing, barely avoiding the
giant claws. Above, men standing on the metal platforms
directed high-pressure hoses at the mud and rocks dumped
there, pushing the material down ramps of metallic mesh

covered in sacks soaked in mercury. The force of the water spread the mud over this grid, so that gold particles would stick to the cloth. Mercury-laden water ran down the legs of these structures onto the ground.

Despite these conditions, the miners displayed no ill humor, just a dogged determination to make the most of this chance. We learned that local people had the right to keep whatever gold they could scoop out by hand during three hours in the morning. On a rotating schedule, the inhabitants of Zaragoza and of nearby villages got access to the pit. With luck one could earn some four hundred dollars a month, decent money for rural areas.

Whichever armed group owned this operation ruled both through violence and through a social compact allowing the community also to benefit from the mine. We had seen this same relationship between armed groups and local communities along other rivers. The compact would last for as long as it took the backhoes, working 24 hours a day, to extract all the gold from the site.

Alluvial mining by backhoe. La Porquera, Zaragoza, Antioquia, 2011.

Gold mine. La Porquera, 2011.

Miner. La Porquera, 20II. -->

Backhoe. La Porquera, 2011.

Backhoe. La Porquera, 20II. -->

OPERATION TROY
=================

The day before the action the journalists arrived at the army's XI Brigade headquarters in Montería, the staging ground for Operation Troy. This multi-year offensive aimed to close gold mines accused of financing both leftist insurgents and Emerging Criminal Bands (BACRIM), as the government labels the militias descended from paramilitary groups that are active in many parts of the country.

After a briefing, the base commander took them to the war room to see an enormous map of the region on a table, featuring hundreds of colored markers. Each color indicated the presence of Revolutionary Armed Forces of Colombia (FARC) or of National Liberation Army (ELN) leftist guerrillas, or of BACRIM such as the Urabeños (also known as the Clan Úsuga or the Gaitanist Self-Defense Forces of Colombia), the Paisas, or the Rastrojos. The one constant underlying this dizzying array of forces was gold, which had become the main source of financing for all these armed groups.

Before daybreak the next day, troops assembled in formation, while their officers met for a last-minute meeting. Looking at a map made up of rocks placed on the ground and lines drawn in the dirt, they went over the exact location of the mine they planned to raid.

The journalists then boarded one of two helicopters which would transport a squad of heavily armed police towards the Bajo Cauca region of Antioquia. They flew over a landscape of vast ranches dotted with herds of white cattle and with almost no people in sight. The distribution of land and income in Colombia is one of the most unequal in Latin America, and in this region rural day laborers earn some six dollars a day. This extreme inequality forms the background to the armed conflict that has beset Colombia for over fifty years, a conflict funded by resources such as coca, emeralds, bananas, oil and, more recently, gold.

As the helicopters neared El Bagre, Antioquia, the landscape below transformed into a pitted panorama of diverted streams, heaps of discarded tailings, and pools filled with stagnant water turned green and orange by chemical runoff.

The helicopters landed in the middle of this lunar realm, disgorging troops, representatives of the Attorney General's office, regional environmental authorities and several TV crews. The police ran towards a large backhoe and attempted to arrest the two men who had been operating the machinery. Immediately a large crowd formed, many brandishing sticks, and a brief tug-of-war occurred. The police, vastly outnumbered, were forced to release their captives. One young man watching the struggle said to a policeman, "at least the guerrillas let us work." The officer angrily pointed his finger at the youth, and retorted, "that is subversive thinking!"

Police, Operation Troy. XI Brigade. Montería,
Córdoba, 2011.

Bajo Cauca region, Antioquia, 2011.

Operation Troy. El Bagre, Antioquia, 2011.

"That is subversive thinking!" El Bagre, 2011.

THE VEIN
========

Gold's average concentration in the earth's crust is .0005 grams/metric ton (g/t). Silver has a concentration of .07 g/t, and copper has a concentration of 50 g/t. So gold occurs only rarely in comparison to other economically valuable metals. According to the U.S. Geological Survey, all the gold mined in the world so far would fit into a cube 22 meters on each side.

Underground gold deposits are formed by the action of water, pressure, or magma that pushed gold towards the surface of the earth millions of years ago. Once the gold cooled it tended to occupy the cracks in other minerals, forming veins of ore. Such gold deposits frequently occur in areas with greater geological activity, such as those near tectonic faults.

The veins in the gold mines in the Segovia-Remedios mining district are part of the Segovia Gold Belt, a region of volcanic rocks measuring approximately 300 km in length by up to 75 km in width, which was formed in the late Jurassic period between 160 and 145 million years ago. Gold in the Segovia belt occurs in lenticular (thick in the middle and thin on both edges, like a lens) veins, in a quartz matrix. It is also associated with pyrite, chalcopyrite, sphalerite, and galena. Miners look for brown pyrite crystals, which they call *cacao*, to help them locate the ore.

Traditional miners in the Segovia-Remedios region extract the gold from this matrix with pneumatic drills and dynamite, and they carry it out in sacks called *catangas*.

Each year in Segovia, as part of the Festival of the Virgin of Carmen and Gold Mining, miners compete in a race carrying 50 kilos of rock in one of these sacks. One miner told Stephen that the race was far easier than the actual work in Segovia's mines, where miners have to carry that weight while crouching and climbing through narrow, winding tunnels.

In these photographs from Segovia and Marmato, we can see how miners hack, crack, ponder, pick over, strain, and shove to wrest gold from the earth's tight mineral grip.

Gold vein. La Roca mine, Segovia, Antioquia, 2012.

Segovia, 2012.

La Roca mine, Segovia, 2012.

La Roca mine, Segovia, 20I2.

La Roca mine, Segovia, 2012. -->

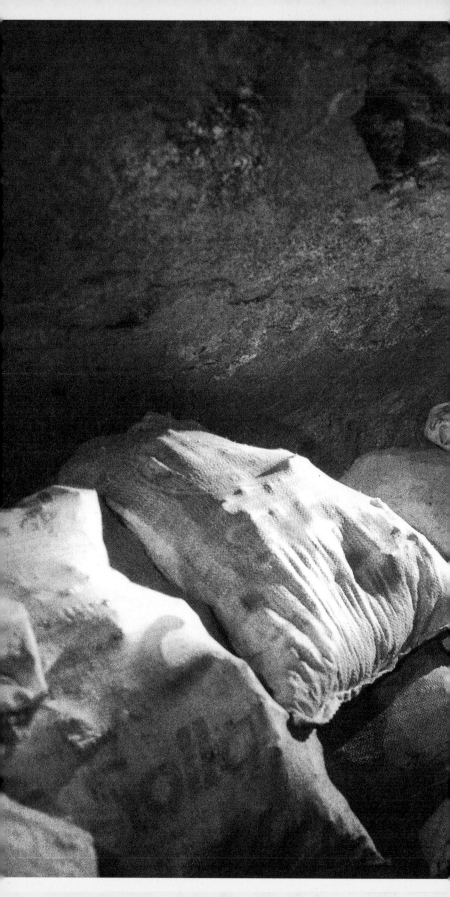

Miner carries ore-bearing rocks in a catanga.
Segovia, 2016.

Gold vein. Marmato, Caldas, 2017 -->

LA CHATARRERA
============

The word *chatarrera* in Spanish refers to a female junkyard worker. But in the context of traditional mining it refers to a centuries-old custom by which miners leave some material by the side of the mine, so that others, usually women, can pick through and break it up to recover the gold within. These are the rocks that miners remove when they dynamite open the tunnels and galleries in which to work veins of gold. They contain gold, in smaller quantities than the vein itself.

In his account *Voyage to the New World: 1599-1605*, Friar Diego de Ocaña describes how in the mines of Potosí (in present-day Bolivia) "the Indian women look for rocks that are discarded around the mouth of the mine, which is called *pallar*, that is to break them up and choose those of value and separate them from the rest." Even today, the miners of Potosí discard tailings so that the *pailliris*, widows of deceased miners, have a chance to earn a living from the mine. In 1785, a Spanish official, Fernando Márquez in Huancavelica (in what is now Peru), observed a similar practice, known there as *pallaqueo*, in which indigenous men, women, and children picked over the surface materials and took them to miners to be processed.

When we first visited the La Roca mine in Segovia in 2012, the owners proudly showed us their chatarrera, in which some 250 women worked, many of them widows of Colombia's internal armed conflict. But by 2016, this chatarrera had disappeared, as La Roca was obliged to sign an operating contract with the Gran Colombia Gold corporation or risk eviction at the hands of the police. The contract requires that La Roca deliver all its production to be processed by Gran Colombia Gold. This is in keeping with the corporation's modern business model that privileges efficiency, thus leaving the chatarreras, and all who depend on them, out of the picture.

Chatarrera. La Roca mine, Segovia, Antioquia, 2012.

Chatarrera. Mina Nueva, Antioquia, 2016. -->

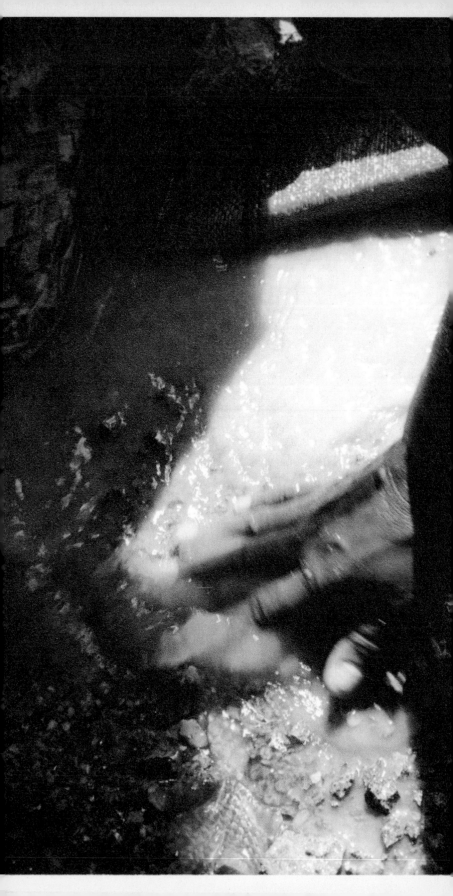

MERCURY
=======

The Romans revered the god Mercury as a swift–footed
messenger crossing boundaries at will, a master thief, and
the patron of trade. Little wonder that the liquid metal,
also known as quicksilver, should be named for the trickster
god. Beautiful and slippery, mercury has the uncanny ability
to separate gold and silver particles from their geological
context, teasing out the precious ore trapped within rocks
and mud. Just as the god Mercury rescued beautiful
Proserpina from the Underworld, so does the metal mercury
extract beauty from the darkness and dirt.

But, true to its trickster nature, mercury is also a curse.
The element remains perpetually in the environment, cycling
between vapor and liquid. Microorganisms in water convert
it to methylmercury, which is more toxic still and which
lodges in the fat of those who consume it. As creatures eat
other creatures the poison is transported up the food chain
and ultimately into us. A powerful toxin, mercury affects
the body's organs and attacks the nervous system, causing
sexual impotence, tremors, personality changes, insanity, and
death.

Heavy exposure to mercury can also cause birth defects,
as documented by W. Eugene Smith's 1975 photographic
essay published in *LIFE* magazine, which exposed the
devastating effects of mercury contamination on the fishing
community of Minamata, Japan. The Chisso fertilizer
manufacturer dumped methylmercury into the Minamata

Bay over decades, ultimately killing more than 900 people and causing widespread cerebral palsy and other deformities. Mercury poisoning is now often called Minamata Disease.

People in the gold mining regions of northeastern Antioquia may be the most exposed to mercury in the world. In 2010, the levels of mercury vapor in the streets of Segovia were found to be a thousand times higher than the safety limits defined by the World Health Organization. Since then, the vapor levels have gone down thanks to refineries that installed retorts, a device that can capture and recycle much of the mercury before it escapes. Nonetheless, this region still releases some 75 tons of the element into the environment each year.

Along with 127 other nations, Colombia has signed the 2013 Minamata Convention, pledging to eliminate mercury use in the near future. But many miners and refinery workers in Colombia, like millions of small-scale miners the world over, continue to use it. Mercury is inexpensive and useful to the subsistence miner. And since mercury poisoning occurs gradually, it is not immediately evident even in a place as contaminated as Segovia. Nevertheless, toxicological research confirms that many persons in Segovia have heightened levels of mercury in their bodies, and several small-scale studies suggest that early symptoms of mercury poisoning, such as memory loss, tremors and agitation, may be widespread. Indeed, when a motorcyclist races through the streets of Segovia at high speed, he is said to be *azogado*, under the effects of *azogue*, an old-fashioned term for mercury.

Still, many Segovians are skeptical about the risk, and the necessities of daily life and generations of custom take precedence over what seems to be an abstract concern. Some refinery owners view the prohibition against mercury as merely a corporate and government plot to get rid of them.

Meanwhile, in over a hundred refineries located in Segovia and Remedios, miners bring in sacks of ore-bearing rocks and dump them into spherical mills, known as *cocos*. An operator adds manganese balls, mercury, honey, and lime or orange rinds and set the cocos spinning for four hours so the manganese can grind up the rocks and the other substances cause the gold particles to stick together. After that, the operator pours out the sludge, which the miner then sluices by hand in a batea, adding more mercury. Next, he takes a piece of nylon and squeezes this concentrate of gold and mercury into a tight wad, the *amalgama*. Using a blowtorch, the miner then burns off the mercury, revealing a ball of gold ready for sale.

Large-scale mining companies—such as Gran Colombia Gold—argue that their processing methods are more ecologically sound than those of traditional miners because, instead of mercury, they process ore with cyanide and neutralize its toxicity before disposing of it. Gran Colombia Gold has its own refinery in Segovia and demands that all the gold mined within its concession be processed there.

But there are many examples of traditional miners throughout Colombia who manage without quicksilver. One refinery owner in Segovia is developing an alternative using gravel as a filtration system. In Marmato, Caldas, traditional miners generally frown on the use of mercury. They rely on grinding machines, cyanide treatment plants, slanted shaking tables which sort out gold through gravity, and on their skillful use of the batea. Along the Pacific coast of Colombia, many indigenous and Afro-Colombian alluvial miners also decline to use mercury.

The survival of the traditional mining sector in Segovia may well depend on these alternatives, as world-wide pressure to ban mercury is only likely to increase.

Cocos. Los Guaduales refinery, Segovia, Antioquia, 2013.

Los Guaduales refinery, Segovia, 2012.

Mercury and gold in batea. Segovia, 2013. -->

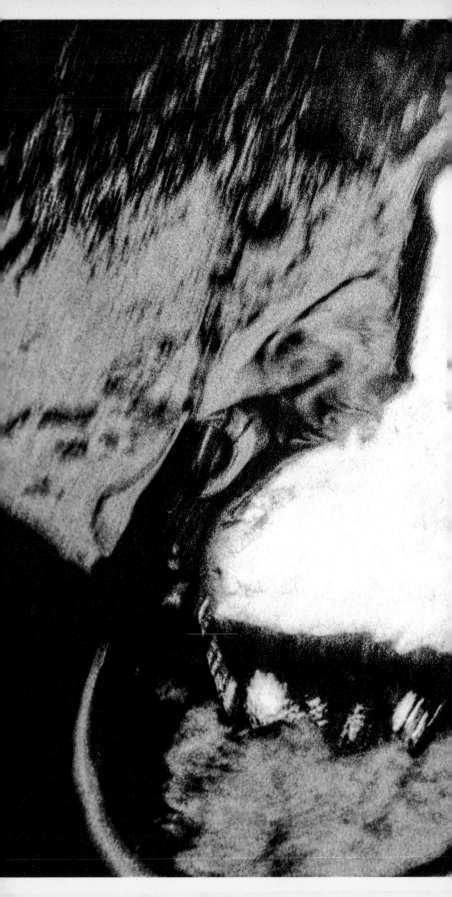

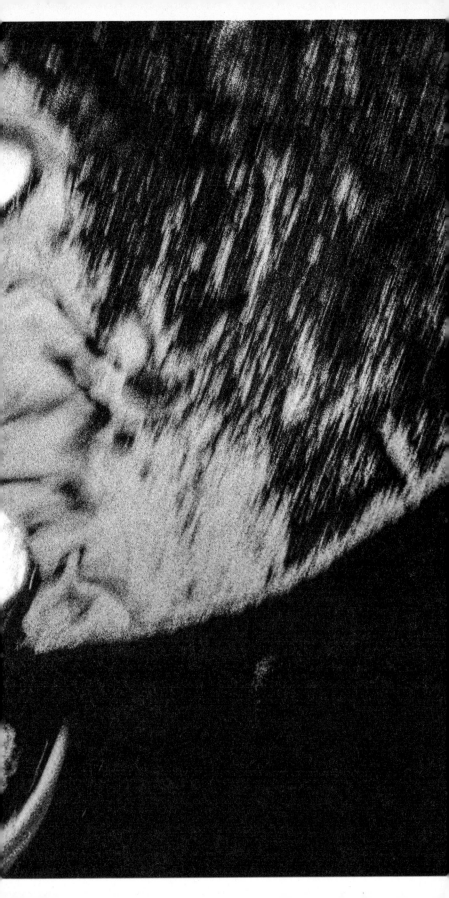

Miner squeezes mercury and gold amalgam with nylon.
Segovia, 2012.

Amalgam of mercury and gold. Segovia, 2012. --> -->

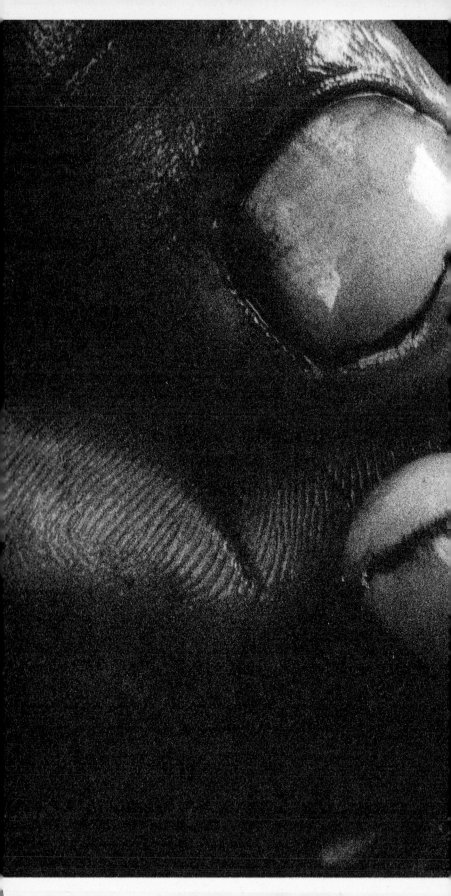

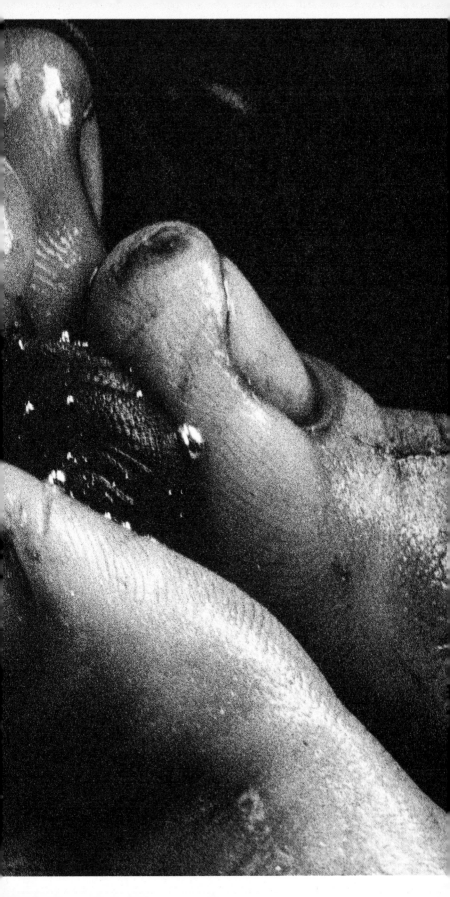

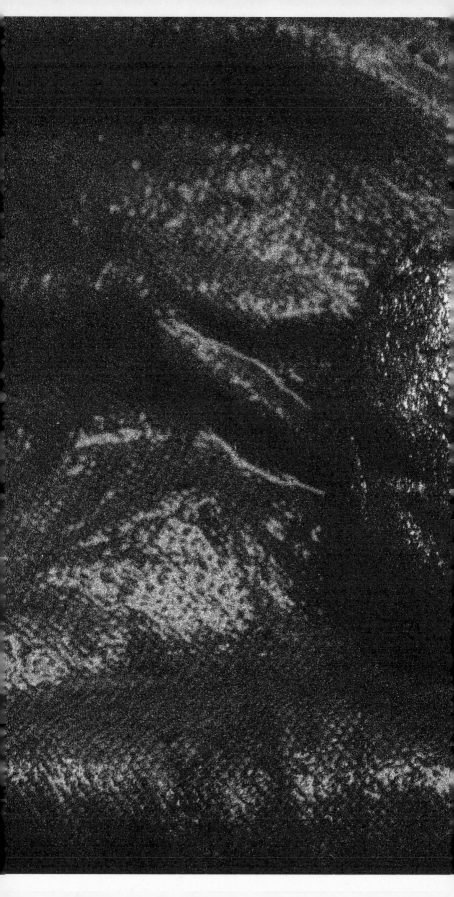

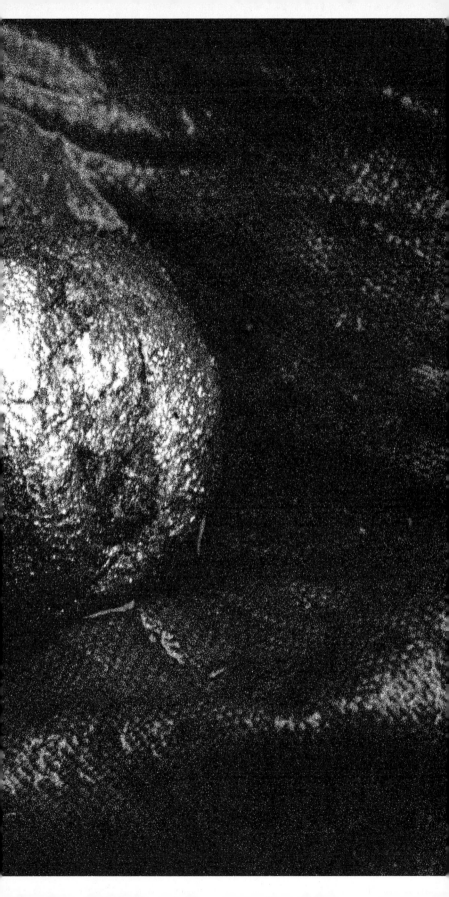

A STATUE IN SEGOVIA

The monument towers over the main plaza of Segovia, Antioquia, which, along with next-door Remedios, is the principal mining region of Colombia. Entirely painted in gold, the statue depicts a naked woman, her ankles and wrists in shackles, raising a batea up to the sky. Her face is contorted in a grimace, as a miner hammers at her womb. He has split her open, revealing a lode of golden rocks jaggedly showing through the torn flesh.

In contrast with the dramatic motif of the statue, Segovians sit around its base chatting, while their children frolic in the small plaza. Others frequent the "kiosko," an open-air café a few steps away, where meetings are held, gossip is shared, and people tease one another in the way that only old friends can. This difference between foreground and background sums up the contradictions of Segovia, a city with a notoriously violent history that also prides itself on being festive, welcoming to outsiders, and hard-working.

Just a few steps away there is another monument, a small plaque to honor the victims of the massacre of 1988, when paramilitary forces working with the army and police killed 43 civilians in the streets around this plaza. This massacre was one of many that characterized Colombia's internal war. For over half a century, left-wing guerrilla armies—the Revolutionary Armed Forces of Colombia (FARC) and the National Liberation Army (ELN)—have fought against the Colombian state and allied right-wing militias, known as paramilitaries. (In 2016, the FARC signed a peace treaty with the Colombian government.) Civilians, such as the miners of Segovia-Remedios, have borne the brunt of the conflict, as the warring parties contend for resources and rent.

To get an idea how gold has defined Segovia and Remedios, for better and for worse, we must look at the history of the Frontino mine complex, the oldest, the largest employer and the greatest producer of gold and silver in the region. Founded in 1852 by English miners, who brought with them important technologies such as the steam engine, the Frontino and Bolivia Company had a reputation for fair treatment of its workers, offering good salaries and food subsidies to offset the high cost of living typical of mining regions. In 1910, the International Mining Corporation from the USA bought the company and changed its name to Frontino Gold Mines.

In 1977, after years of low gold prices, labor conflict and hostile actions by leftist guerrillas, the U.S. owners of Frontino Gold Mines declared themselves unable to meet the pension obligations of the company. As a way to pay this debt, the company signed over ownership to Frontino's workers on condition that Frontino would maintain a solvent pension fund.

In the following period, the price of gold climbed and the Frontino mines remained the main source of employment in the region, continuing to provide the benefits and services to its workers demanded by labor unions, as well as maintaining a hospital for the community. Yet the Frontino mines were also chronically mismanaged. Armed groups on both sides of the conflict extorted money from Frontino and infiltrated its facilities.

In the 1980s, a paramilitary group calling itself Death to Revolutionaries of the Northeast moved into Segovia to take control of the mines, rid the city of guerrillas, and assassinate social leaders, leftist politicians and trade unionists who they viewed as subversives. For their part, the FARC and the ELN organized urban militias that extorted local businesses for "war taxes" and attacked their perceived civilian enemies. In the years 1982-1997 Segovia suffered 14 massacres at the hands of paramilitaries and state forces, and 200 more political murders carried out by all parties to the conflict. Paramilitaries allied with state forces ultimately prevailed and guerrilla forces largely withdrew to the rural areas around Segovia.

On several occasions, the paramilitaries organized extended campaigns to steal ore from the Frontino company. They mobilized hundreds of miners, known as *machuqueros*, who occupied tunnels deep within Frontino's mining complex, living underground for weeks and processing the ore on-site using bicycle-driven grinders to sneak the gold out undetected. One veteran of these campaigns told how the machuqueros would invite prostitutes into the tunnels, paying for their services with gold nuggets. Mine officials were either complicit or powerless to prevent these invasions.

In 2004, Colombian president Alvaro Uribe began proceedings to liquidate and sell Frontino, arguing that the company never organized the promised pension fund. Uribe offered Frontino to the Gran Colombia Gold Corporation in 2010 for close to 200 million dollars on the condition that the multinational pay the pensions. Gran Colombia Gold soon laid off much of the permanent work force. Seeking to keep ownership of the mine in the hands of workers, leaders of the miners' trade union Sintramienergetica took the case to the courts. At this time, they received numerous death threats and union leader Jhon Jairo Zapata was shot three times in the stomach by a hired gunman.

Many in Segovia see the sale of the Frontino mine as a massive robbery of their patrimony backed by paramilitary violence. Opponents point out that the first president of the Gran Colombia Corporation, María Consuelo Araujo, belongs to a powerful political clan with proven links to paramilitaries in her home province of Cesar. In an interview, Araujo emphatically denied that Gran Colombia Gold played any role in the attacks on trade unionists in Segovia.

Given this background, we read the statue in the central plaza as a reference to this violent history. But when we asked Heliodoro Álvarez, a miner with deep roots in Segovia, his interpretation, he responded:

We dig in the organs, in the internal parts of Mother Earth.
She lets us tunnel within her womb, to give us sustenance.
No matter how much we crush her, she does not say
anything, she keeps on offering us what we need to eat.
She represents a mother, as with a mother and child, at
times the child makes her suffer greatly, yet she does not
stop being the mother and the child does not stop being
the child, and each day she loves him more.

Heliodoro Álvarez knows about digging for gold. After
prospecting for over a year with his son, he discovered
a rich vein some 300 meters underneath the July 20th
neighborhood of Segovia. With members of his extended
family, Álvarez organized the La Roca mine, which was soon
taking out over 500,000 dollars worth of gold per month. In
2012, he proudly showed Stephen the mine, explaining that
he employed over 70 workers.

But then Álvarez's good fortune turned to tragedy. As
documented by journalist Nadja Drost, a band of veteran
paramilitaries known as the Heroes of the Northeast,
claimed La Roca's ore as theirs. To make their point they
killed two members of Álvarez's family and two other
associates in an ambush. At the same time, the Heroes were
at war with another neo-paramilitary band, known as the
Urabeños, for control of Segovia's mines.

As this war intensified, hundreds of civilians were killed
in Segovia and Remedios. La Roca hired Javier Cardona, a

tough and canny veteran of the Colombian conflict, to run security for the mine. When Drost asked him if La Roca was paying the Urabeños to protect them against their mutual enemy, Cardona declared that if any associate of La Roca were to do that, he would personally cut off his head. He said he preferred to wage war using intelligence, organizing a network of informants to provide information on the Heroes to the police. Ultimately, the Urabeños gained control of Segovia, and the La Roca mine remained in the hands of Heliodoro Álvarez's family.

As of 2017, with their rivals defeated, the Urabeños are killing fewer people in Segovia. They extort tribute from mines throughout Segovia and Remedios, and their insignia is painted on the walls of many neighborhoods, along with messages threatening informants with death.

All the while, in the central plaza, kids frolic around the base of the statue as their parents sip coffee in the afternoon sunshine.

Segovia, Antioquia, 2013.

Javier Cardona, chief of security of La Roca mine.
Segovia, 2013. -->

Security detail, La Roca mine, Segovia, 2013.

July 20th neighborhood, close to the La Roca Mine.
Segovia, 2013. -->

Bodyguard of trade unionist practices his aim.
Segovia, 2012.

Trade unionist Jhon Jairo Zapata recuperates after
assassination attempt. Safe house, undisclosed
location, 20II. -->

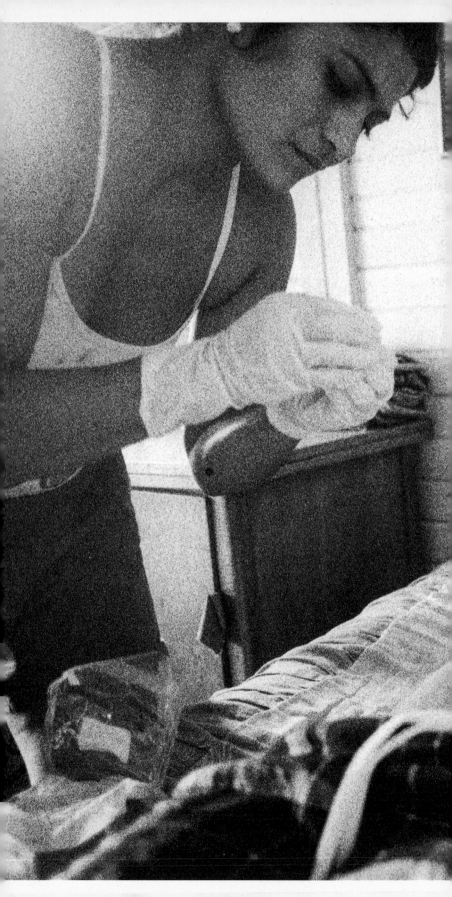

Office of Sintramienergetica trade union, with
pictures of assassinated leaders. Segovia, 2012.

Police patrol. Segovia, 2012.

III

THE STRIKE

The first day was slow. Few people showed up in the early morning at the dusty crossroads known as the Electrificadora that served as headquarters for the general strike. We walked down there with Medardo Tejada, a local journalist we had hired as a guide to help navigate the tricky terrain of Segovia's mining conflicts. Medardo is a rail-thin man with a kind disposition who was once mayor of Segovia—the "stupidest mayor in Segovia's history," he laughingly announced, because he "did not steal."

Seeing how few people had congregated around the tents set up by the striking miners, Medardo was worried. He said that even though all the businesses of Segovia and Remedios had closed in support of the strike, without the presence of miners on the street the protest could fail.

The strike had been called in reaction to a decree from the National Mining Agency threatening prison for anyone processing gold without a certificate from a legally titled mine. For many miners in Segovia and Remedios, this was just the most recent of many governmental actions that favored the multinational Gran Colombia Gold corporation over their interests. When Gran Colombia Gold acquired the Frontino concession in 2010, the company insisted that any existing mines within its more than 16,000 hectare concession had to sign operating contracts or be subject to eviction by the police. Many traditional miners objected that with these contracts the multinational receives over 60% of the value of their production, despite the fact that they and their ancestors had built these mines decades before the arrival of Gran Colombia Gold on the scene. The region's miners also protested that these are short-term contracts that could lead to their mines' expropriation by Gran Colombia Gold.

The Colombian state, which leases the subsoil, views these operating contracts as negotiations between private parties that should proceed without state involvement. In an interview several months before the strike with Dr. Enrique Olano Asuad, Secretary of Mines of Antioquia, we asked about the situation in Segovia. He argued that the company was within its rights to decide the terms of the contract, as Segovia's miners were "like people squatting in someone else's apartment." For its part, Gran Colombia Gold maintains that these contracts offer local miners the opportunity to formalize their claims and adopt technically modern methods with company guidance.

As the first day of the strike wore on, a group of chatarrera workers from the Las Brisas mine set up a communal kitchen and some men showed up with sides of beef to feed the strikers. Jaime Gallego, a leader of the Negotiating Table of Traditional and Ancestral Miners of Segovia and Remedios (Mesa Minera), stood on a makeshift podium and exhorted Segovia's gold miners to participate in the strike. He joked that even though many miners would likely still have a hangover from the previous night's excesses, they had to show up anyway to defend their community and their rights as "ancestral" gold miners. As the leaders took turns speaking to the growing crowd, over and over again they emphasized the word "ancestral."

The organizers repeatedly instructed the small crowd to keep calm, not to provoke the police, and to allow all emergency vehicles to pass through the roadblocks set up throughout Segovia and Remedios. At one point, they distributed balloons to the hundred or so people gathered in the crossroads, asking people to release them all together in memory of William García Cartagena, a legal adviser to the miners who was assassinated on the day the miners' strike was announced. García Cartagena had been subject to threats for his work with the miners, and the timing left little doubt that it was a message meant to intimidate the strikers. The grim faces of people as they watched the incongruously festive balloons float upwards into the hazy sky testified that more blood might well be spilled.

Over the next few days, traffic came to a halt and businesses remained closed, including the saloons and dance halls that usually pulse with *vallenato* and reggaeton music at all hours. More people gathered each day to hear organizers shouting updates on the progress of talks with the governor's office. The Mesa Minera was demanding that the government provide protection to threatened mining leaders and that Gran Colombia Gold return to the bargaining table.

On the fourth day of the strike, Gran Colombia Gold made a public relations error. The vice-president of the corporation, José Ignacio Noguera, complained in a radio interview that the strike was costing the company two million dollars a day, suggesting that the foreign-based company was taking out over half a billion dollars of gold a year from the veins underneath Segovia and Remedios. Also, CEO Lombardo Paredes declared that "these are not our workers who are on strike, but simply a group of bandits around there who have kidnapped the population." After hearing these statements, many indignant Segovians joined the strikers on the street, and the City Council of Segovia issued a statement denouncing these declarations.

The strong reaction to these statements by Gran Colombia Gold was not only because people felt insulted, but also because in Colombia the term "bandits" is often used to stigmatize the opposition as guerrillas, and thus to justify acts of violence. In 2010, the Sintramienergetica union protested that Serafino Iacono, a major shareholder of Medoro (now Gran Colombia Gold), had incited a climate of intimidation days before the attack on unionist Jhon Jairo Zapata, by allegedly referring to the union as guerrillas.

On the sixth day, the riot police showed up early in the morning at the Electrificadora to clear the roadblocks and occupy the tents which served as headquarters for the strike. At this, the streets around began to fill with angry miners and a violent clash between the riot police and the crowd broke out. The objective of the police—firing teargas, rubber bullets and glass marbles—was to hold the tents and thus break the strike; that of the miners—throwing rocks and advancing slowly as a bloc—was to retake them. Ambulances came and went.

In the end, the miners won. As hundreds of people finally advanced on the police, men and women in the front lines linked arms to prevent a stampede that could easily have caused deaths on both sides. As the mass of people bore down on the outnumbered troops, the police suddenly retreated from the area, gasping from their own teargas. There were 36 wounded, but no fatalities. The strike organizers were elated as they took to the podium to resume the strike and call once again for calm. One young woman, beaming from ear to ear, turned to Stephen and asked, "Did you film the revolution?"

Five days later, the strike was lifted, after Antioquia's Governor's Office insisted that Gran Colombia Gold renew negotiations with the miners. The Mesa Minera optimistically said, "there is a recognition by the institutions of our knowledge as ancestral and traditional miners."

Yet, as of mid-2017, the death threats continue. On May 10th, a group calling itself "The Hand that Cleans" distributed a flyer with the image of a pistol, stating that "As of today we declare every organizer of marches, protests and public meetings to be a military target. To the Mesa Minera: we have already warned that you must stop agitating the people."

Miners' strike. Segovia, Antioquia, 2016.

Communal kitchen for striking miners. Segovia, 2016.

Miners' strike. Segovia, 2016.

Riot police in retreat. Segovia, 2016.

THE GIANTESS
============

In the middle of the revel, Stephen was approached by Angel Cuessi, a large man wearing a jester's cap. He introduced himself, laughingly, as the "organizer of this disorder." Cuessi explained that in the 1980s, a group of musicians brought La Gigantona (The Giantess) from nearby Zaragoza to Segovia to enrich the yearly Festival of the Virgin of Carmen and Gold Mining. Segovians adopted La Gigantona with all their characteristic fervor.

According to legend, the giant figure represents a miner, said to have been a tall, sexy woman who flirted with every man she came across. La Gigantona would show up each year in nearby Zaragoza to sell the gold she had collected by panning in nearby rivers. She used the money she earned to hire a band of musicians and buy enough liquor to throw a huge party right there in the port of Zaragoza, before leaving once more upriver.

Roots of the festival reach back to Imperial Spain, and there is another Gigantona festival in León, Nicaragua. Like carnivals throughout the Americas, La Gigantona upends the established order of society. Rather than being a respectful procession in honor of the Virgin, this revel is an uninhibited display of lusty adoration for a sexual woman who loved to party.

At the end of the procession, the young miners who were carrying The Giantess began running her back and forth, ultimately toppling her over and emerging laughing from under her skirts. One man declared possessively that "she is my girlfriend." Another kissed her cheek. And another pretended to penetrate her from behind, wielding a cow bone as a phallus. The gathered revelers, faces and bodies painted with blackberry juice, laughed appreciatively at the bacchanalian scene.

La Gigantona is a fitting saint for Segovia, a town where many gold miners easily spend their hard-earned money on liquor, parties, and sex.

La Gigantona. Segovia, Antioquia, 2016.

La Gigantona. Segovia, 2016.

La Gigantona. Segovia, 2016.

HOUSEHOLD GOD

Gold melts above 1,064 degrees Celsius. The kiln that melts this gold, in the Molino El Arco, is hotter still. It is so hot its flames turn not to red or white, but green. They curl like new spring ferns. The heat seems to shock the air and the air to empty out and wait. It feels as though at any moment the space around the kiln might yield and swirl into a world of fire. It feels as though the earth and mill and kiln and all of us around the kiln might turn to stars.

There is a man next to the kiln, all bundled up in boots and heavy gloves and mask and thick, misted visor. The kiln, squat and grey, with one burning eye in the middle of its lid, is tilted forward and just about to puke out molten gold. The man is waiting to do what he needs to do when the gold pours out.

The kiln is housed in a shed built from brick and concrete, divided in two. On one side, some bags of material, an empty shelf, a sign on the wall. Nobody there. On the other side, the man and the kiln.

From one point of view, the kiln is entirely mechanical and each part makes sense. The man seems almost an extension of the machine, though the curve of his shoulders and his hand's position are unmistakably alive and human. But from another point of view, the kiln is a squat, grinning little household god and the man is its priest and caretaker. He has to make sure it is fed and satisfied, or it will spill its nasty temper all around us.

And the earth and mill and kiln and all of us around the kiln will turn to stars.

El Arco refinery, Marmato, Caldas, 2013.

Molten gold. Marmato, 2013. -->

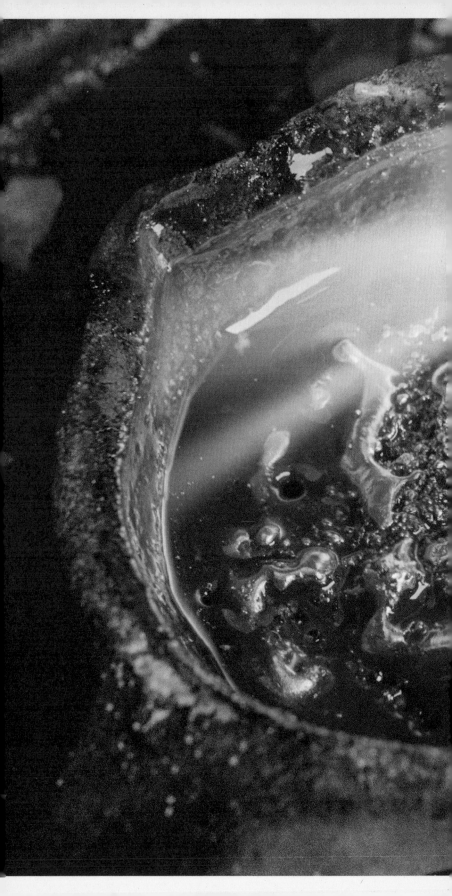

MARMATO
=======

At a level part of the town of Marmato, there is a line of
small-scale gold mills, each with a bustling crew of a dozen
or so people. At one end, a row of motorcycles stands next to
bags of rock and gravel. We are sitting on one of these bags,
in the warm morning sun, looking up the hill. Down the side
runs a sliding slope of rocks and in the middle of these rocks
we can see small shelters or stations made out of timber.
These lean-tos set into the slope are dispatch points where
miners load the ore. Some are slanting over—one has given
up the ghost and been crushed. Every few minutes a rock or
two is dislodged and falls.

  A few yellow signs warn of the danger of falling rocks.
Between the structures on the level part of the hillside,
where we are sitting, and the platforms higher up runs
an elaborate system of zip-lines spanning hundreds of
meters. Along these cables come whizzing little buckets
that whistle and chirp as they slide along the metal like
Industrial Age R2D2s. Their noise mixes with the sounds of
the chattering morning birds. Down the mountain go the
buckets, full of ore, and empty into concrete chutes that
feed into the mills below. Back up the mountain they go,
their bottoms open and flapping a little. They are painted
school bus yellow or maybe gold, a few freshly and others
years ago.

  The residents of Marmato have been mining gold
since before the arrival of the Spanish, and the area has

been mined by the native Cartama people, the Spanish, the British, the Colombians, and now by the Canadians. In 1946, the upper zone of the mountain was set aside for small- and medium-scale mining and has become the site of a flourishing, somewhat chaotic-seeming economy, with hundreds of mines and mills piled on top of each other.

The boom in gold prices that started in the early 2000s and picked up steam after the world financial crisis has threatened a radical change in Marmato's topography. As prices rose and as the Colombian internal conflict became less active in the 2000s, transnational mining companies began moving into historic mining districts in Colombia, including Marmato. The multinational Gran Colombia Gold has conducted exploration in the Marmato district, estimating that nearly 14 million ounces of gold lie in the mountain.

Gran Colombia Gold has also been buying up mining titles in the upper areas of the El Burro mountain, on which Marmato stands, with an eye to digging an open-pit mine that would remove the top of the mountain, including the historic town of Marmato, relocate its residents to a lower level and exploit most of the minable gold over the next twenty years. A number of residents in the upper zone have sold their mines to the company, but those who oppose the project—organized into the Association of Traditional Miners of Marmato—cite the destructive effects of open-pit mining on the environment and the loss of a way of life dating back centuries.

The company and the national press depict Marmato as a place that needs to be rescued from the gold fever that has caused it to consume itself. On October 10, 2011, the newspaper *Portafolio* reported that in this place where we are sitting and watching the day wake up and start to work, "an avalanche carried off the town hall, plaza, church and ninety-two houses." The weekly news magazine *Semana* told this story as "The Disgrace of Marmato," noting that "gold fever has its dangers." However, when Stephen first visited Marmato in 2013, he found the reports of the avalanche to be greatly exaggerated; the town had not dug out its very foundations in a fit of greed.

Still it is true that there have been reports since the early 1980s of structural instability of the areas around the mines, suggesting the possibility of a massive collapse due to the criss-crossing tunnels that have been dug beneath the surface over centuries. These reports call for various solutions, from the immediate cessation of mining in the area, to relocation of the town, to projects for mitigation and education. Yet, the state has invested little effort and resources to improve the structural instabilities that do exist.

Given the controversy over Gran Colombia's plans for the mountain, the question of Marmato's instability has become a proxy for whether or not open-pit mining should proceed. Those who support Gran Colombia's plans are not likely to argue for shoring up the mountain so that Marmateños can stay where they are. And, those who oppose the plans are more likely to underestimate the risks of staying, because to admit danger has become tantamount to agreeing that the town should be moved.

However, Marmato is not a frozen, lifeless pile of rocks. It is a living town with a past and present, and, many residents hope, a future. It is at once crumbling and thriving with industry. The yellow buckets that we watched zipping about that morning at the mills capture something of the spirit of the town. They are makeshift but highly functional, industrious, and cheerful. They may look like inefficient remnants of an earlier age, but they are still there and still working.

Many people in Marmato told us that some of the town's structures may be shaky, but the social fabric is stronger than in other cities and towns in Colombia. In part this is because of the high employment rate in the mining economy. One resident told us, "You can't get your shoes shined in Marmato, because everyone has a better job than shining shoes." Notably, Marmato has kept itself relatively separate from the internal armed conflict. Neither the guerrillas nor the paramilitaries were able to recruit many combatants, spies, or collaborators in Marmato.

Since we sat on those bags of gravel in January 2013, the situation has changed. The price of gold has now fallen somewhat and the open-pit project in Marmato is apparently on hold. Nonetheless, Gran Colombia Gold continues to seek the eviction of miners who have re-entered 68 mines in the upper zone. The corporation had earlier bought and then closed down these mines in preparation for the open-pit mine.

When we visited Marmato in August 2016, the opposition to Gran Colombia Gold has become more organized, getting candidates elected to local government, working with national and international organizations, and sponsoring a yearly conference of "Marmatologists" to promote research and education about the town's past and present. They are also developing tourism projects, including an educational mine where visitors can enter a tunnel rich in gold veins and see gold mining in action.

In February 2017, the traditional miners of Marmato received a favorable decision from Colombia's Constitutional Court, which ruled that a process of prior consultation must take place before Gran Colombia Gold can evict miners. In April, Gran Colombia Gold countered with a $700 million dollar suit against Colombia charging that this decision violates the Colombia-Canada trade agreement. That suit is still pending.

And other questions remain open: how aggressively the company will pursue its claims; whether the miners can perch on their hill for another round of the gold cycle; and whether they will get the help they need to shore up their world.

Marmato, Caldas, 2011.

Marmato, 2011. -->

147

La Villonza mine. Marmato, 2016.

Upper zone of the El Burro mountain, Marmato, 2016.

Mine entrance with ventilation system. Marmato, 2017.

Marmato, 2013.

Wood used to support tunnels. Marmato, 2016.

Marmato, 2016.

TRANSMISSION
=============

The batea is a shallow, concave wooden pan, usually made from cedar. The use of the batea is not an art that can be mastered by just anyone. Indeed, the day we visit, several young men watch and help Amed Amar Osorio through the whole morning as he transmits to them the craft.

It takes several hours to get the gold from even a small quantity of pay dirt, with a constant adding of water, laundry detergent, and a steady shaking and swirling to coax the gold dust out of the surrounding muck so it will fall to the bottom of the pan. Every ten or twenty seconds, Amed stops swirling the batea. He holds his hand just so, so the second and third joints of his fingers can gently and persistently stroke the surface of the water. The swirling and stroking encourage the bits of dirt and rock and gold to spread away from each other horizontally, so that the gold will fall. The laundry soap helps skim off the grease. Every few minutes he pours off some of the water with dirt in it, but not the gold on the bottom.

After some time, we see sparkles in the dirt, but we know enough to know that these sparkles are not gold but pyrite. The gold shows itself much more slowly, as a yellow smear at the bottom of the batea. Once the gold is collected, a tiny pile to emerge from all that mud, it is carefully toasted on a hot plate to burn off a bit more of the dross and then stored away in an envelope until the buyers come later in the day.

Even though this work happens most days, we are not the only ones fascinated by it. There are the boys who are there to learn the craft, but others, too, stop by the mill to sit and watch. There is something mesmerizing about the motion of swirl, stop, stroke, skim, swirl, stop, stroke, skim, all through the morning as the sun heats up the day.

Amed Amar Osorio. Marmato, Caldas, 2014.

Marmato, 2014. --> -->

YOLOMBÓ

We visited Yolombó in the department of Cauca in June 2017. Yolombó is part of a federation of five towns known as the Corregimiento de La Toma, governed by an autonomous community council, as are many Afro-Colombian areas in the Pacific region.

When we asked María Yein Mina about mining in her community, she said, "I'll have to divide my answer into 'before' and 'after' the arrival of the *retros,*" the backhoes that outsiders brought to the Ovejas River beginning in the late 1980s.

Until then, members of the five towns practiced a balanced economy of mining, fishing, and subsistence agriculture along with a few commercial crops such as coffee. People usually worked on the farm on Monday and Tuesday and spent the rest of the week mining and fishing. At first some members of the community fell into the trap of the retros, neglecting their farms in order to mine the strata of gold particles exposed by the machinery in the banks of the Ovejas River. But then they realized that this way led to ruin: the banks were churned up, gold was becoming scarce, and people no longer wanted to swim or fish because of mercury in the water. They petitioned the authorities to enforce environmental laws, without success.

Led by the younger residents of Yolombó, the community went en masse to the river, boarded the machines and compelled the owners to turn them off. In

2014, a group of fifteen women travelled, mostly on foot, to a series of other Afro-Colombian communities also faced with the imposition of mechanized alluvial mining in their territories. Strengthened by numbers, they arrived in Bogotá to pressure the national government to act. The media called their movement "The March of the Turbans," in reference to the wrapped scarves many of the women wore on their heads. They reached out for national and international support.

Their efforts worked, perhaps too well. They had hoped for administrative action that would compel the backhoes' owners to remove them; the police simply showed up and burned the machinery. As a consequence, leaders of the movement received a wave of death threats.

The people of La Toma had to defend their territory on a second front, this one underground. In the early 2000s, the multinational company AngloGold Ashanti began taking core samples in the area, and also sent agents into the community as social workers, festival sponsors and contributors to public works such as repairing the highway. This is a common—and from the corporate perspective, widely accepted—strategy, but one that was viewed with suspicion in the villages of La Toma. Sure enough, they soon learned that the Ministry of Mines had granted mining titles to AngloGold Ashanti and to private citizens with no links to the community. These concessions entailed the removal of the families living there—practically the entire town of La Toma. In 2009, the government sent the police to displace the residents. The community stood its ground, facing security forces with crowbars and machetes in hand.

They also fought back through the courts, filing lawsuits on grounds of loss of livelihood and the lack of prior consultation, in violation of the International Labor Organization convention to which Colombia is a signatory. In 2010, the Constitutional Court accepted their arguments and declared that the mining titles must be suspended. Again, leaders received death threats in the form of pamphlets, phone calls and text messages.

In the face of these threats, residents formed the Maroon Guard. The word maroon refers historically to communities of escaped slaves, but its meaning has expanded to refer to black resistance in Latin America and the Caribbean in its many forms. The Maroon Guard is a community police force of about 40 young men and women, which manages internal conflicts and protects the community from outside threats. They based their movement on the Palenque Police, set up by residents of the historic maroon community of San Basilio de Palenque. The Maroon Guard also shares methods with the Indigenous Guard, an organized force within the nearby reservations of the Nasa people that has confronted leftist guerrillas, right-wing paramilitaries and the state in defense of native territory.

We asked Francia Márquez Mina, lawyer and recipient of the National Prize for the Defense of Human Rights in Colombia if the different guards worked together. She said, "we have different cosmovisions, but yes, we work together in some things."

The families that live in the five towns in the jurisdiction of La Toma—Yolombó, Gelima, El Hato, Dos Aguas and La Toma—have inhabited this region on the Pacific coast of Colombia since the early 17th century, when they were brought as slaves to work the Gelima gold mine and surrounding farms. The gold from Gelima and other smaller mines enriched the city of Popoyán, and the whole Real Audiencia de Quito, which included parts of Southern Colombia, current-day Ecuador, and northern Peru. The Jesuits mainly owned the mines until their expulsion from the Americas in 1767.

Francia Márquez told us that although mining brought their ancestors from Africa as slaves, it also made them free; many bought their liberty by mining for gold in the Ovejas River, while others escaped and lived as maroons. Their families, and the families of those emancipated in the mid-nineteenth century, bought the land from the proceeds of mining and defended it from successive attempts to displace them over the centuries.

When we visited in June 2017, the river was too high for alluvial mining, so we went to an area close to the school in

Yolombó, to see a form of mining called *minería de chorreo* or "water-jet mining." We watched a group of some fifteen miners, members of several families who have owned land in Yolombó for centuries, directing jets of water at the hill to form a channel of red mud at its base. They then use bateas and *almocafres* (a traditional tool shaped like a garden hoe) to separate the gold. Instead of mercury, they use the escoba babosa plant. By these methods, they can mine for decades in the same area, such as this canyon of about fifty-meters diameter. The miners say they sometimes find artifacts left centuries ago in the hillside by their forebears.

The threats have continued. Sent by email from unknown parties, they accuse the community of "opposing progress" and undermining the government's plans for development through foreign investment. For her safety, Francia Márquez no longer lives in the area and travels accompanied by armed bodyguards provided by the state. The community is pressuring authorities to intervene in a mine recently opened by outsiders that is contaminating streams with mercury. AngloGold Ashanti appears to have left the region and its titles have been suspended, but not cancelled. Sabino Lucumí Chocó, president of the La Toma Community Council, calls these titles "a permanent threat" to the survival of the community.

Against this uncertain background, the towns remain organized. Among other things, the community council conducts media relations and legal actions, promotes ancestral culture for youth, and is planning an independent environmental school, to be called "La Batea."

Yolombó, Cauca, 2017.

Miner. Yolombó, 2017.

A WORKSHOP IN MOMPOX
=====================

We arrive at the home and workshop of Flor and Elisa Trespalacios at about 4 pm, having searched all afternoon for artisans who are still working gold in this goldsmithing town. The high price has made it too risky an investment except for custom jobs, and most work is now in silver.

One of the few workshops currently using gold is that of the Trespalacios family, whose patriarch, Luis Guillermo Trespalacios, was one of the most respected artisans of the city. The Trespalacios make all kinds of pieces, but their specialty is *pescaditos*, golden fishes about 10 cm long. Elisa shows us the mold with which the scales are made. She tells us they were the inspiration for the gold fishes made by Aureliano Buendía in Gabriel García Márquez' novel *100 Years of Solitude.* For this is García Márquez country, and indeed Mompox's sunbaked streets and lazy brown river have a dreamy *macondiano* quality—they call to mind the fantastical town of Macondo depicted in that novel. García Márquez once wrote, "Mompox doesn't exist. Sometimes we dream of it, but it doesn't exist."

The house is a large colonial one, with an inside courtyard filled with thick-leaved tropical plants and a parrot who says, "hola" querulously as we walk by. The workspace is at the back of the courtyard and has wooden benches and chairs in front of iron machines for pulling, beating, and molding gold. A custom-made wooden chest stands against the wall. It contains a grid of compartments with dozens of iron tools and implements, all designed by Luis Guillermo Trespalacios and executed by the local ironmonger, who makes his living supplying tools to the goldsmiths in town. We gently touch the iron tools, most only about 10 cm long. Somehow they ask to be weighed in one's hand.

Elisa tells us, "We have his notebooks, they are full of drawings. But many of his ideas were lost. He didn't tell them to us. He didn't want us to go into goldsmithing."

"Why?" we ask.

"Too many men," she laughs gently, a little sadly.

In our time in Mompox, we hear one story twice, about a boy who asked to apprentice to a famous goldsmith. The master sat the boy down at a table in the hot sun, with a bowl of water and spoon and told him to stir. Stir, stir, stir, for hours and hours and hours. If the boy had gotten bored or annoyed, or asked to have a new task, the master would have sent him packing. But he didn't and so he passed the test; he was patient enough to be a goldsmith.

This patience seems to carry over into the town itself, a slow waiting feeling. If gold is too high, they will work silver, using the same techniques, patiently adapting to circumstances till such time as the price falls. When it does, the Mompox goldsmiths will be waiting.

Magdalena river. Mompox, Bolívar, 2014.

Workshop of Flor and Elisa Trespalacios. Mompox, 2014.

Mompox, 2014.

Elisa Trespalacios, Mompox, 2014.

SELECTED SOURCES

ABColombia (2011). *Regalándolo todo: las consecuencias de una política minera no sostenible en Colombia.*

Ángel, M. (2012). "La esclavitud de indígenas y negros en la época colonial," *Semana*, 29 mar.

Applebaum, N. P. (2003). *Muddied waters: Race, Region, and Local History in Colombia, 1846-1948.* Duke University Press.

Arango, M. y Y. Olaya (2012). "Problemática de los pasivos ambientales mineros en Colombia," *Gestión y Ambiente*, No. 15, vol. 3, pp. 125-133. Universidad Nacional de Colombia.

Ararat, L. et al (2013). "La Toma: Historias de territorio, resistencia y autonomía en la cuenca del Alto Cauca." *Observatorio de Territorios Étnicos.* Pontificia Universidad Javeriana.

Báez, F. (2008). *Cronología de la metalurgia colombiana.* Editorial Melvin, Caracas.

Bedoya, M. R. ed. (2017). *Marmato: Disputa por el oro y el territorio.* Biblioteca Vértices Colombianos, Universidad de Antioquia.

Bedoya, A. (2011). *De oro están hechos mis días.* Hombre Nuevo Editores, Medellín.

Botero, C. I. (2012). *El redescubrimiento del pasado prehispánico de Colombia. Viajeros, arqueólogos y coleccionistas (1820-1945).* Universidad de los Andes.

Botero, S. H. (2017). "Minería y contaminación de ríos, las violencias invisibles en el Bajo Cauca," *El Espectador*, 17 ene.

Bryant, S. K. (2006). "Finding Gold, Forming Slavery: The Creation of a Classic Slave Society, Popayan, 1600-1701." *The Americas*, No. 63, vol. 1, pp. 81-112.

Caballero, E. (1970). *Historia económica de Colombia.* Banco de Bogotá. Bogotá.

Caicedo, E. (1971). Historia de las luchas sindicales en Colombia. Ediciones Ceis. Bogotá.

Colmenares, G. (1982). "La economía y la sociedad coloniales 1550-1800." *Manual de historia de Colombia*, vol. 1, pp. 225-300.

Cordy, P. et al, (2011). "Mercury Contamination from Artisanal Gold Mining in Antioquia, Colombia: The World's Highest per Capita Mercury Pollution." *Science of the Total Environment*, No. 410-411, pp. 154-160.

Chávez, Á. (1980). "Arqueología y guaquería," *Revista Javeriana*, No. 12, pp. 335-338.

Child, J. y Arango, M. (1984). *Bancarrotas y crisis. Colombia 1842-1984. América Latina 1981-1984*. Editorial Presencia, Bogotá.

Dietz, K. (2017). "Politics of Scale and Struggles over Mining in Colombia." *Contested Extractivism, Society and the State*, pp. 127-148. Palgrave Macmillan, Reino Unido.

Drost, N. (2014). "The Devil Underground," *The Atavist Magazine*, No. 42.

Echavarría, C. (2014). *"What is legal?" Formalising artisanal and small-scale mining in Colombia*. IIED, London and ARM, Colombia.

Estrada, A. G. y M. G. Rodas (1984). *Historia de Marmato*. Gráficas Cabrera.

Field, L. (2012). "El sistema del oro: exploraciones sobre el destino (emergente) de los objetos de oro precolombino en Colombia," Antipoda: Revista de Antropología y Arqueología (Colombia) 14(1), 67-93.

Fierro, J. (2012). *Políticas mineras en Colombia*. Ilsa, Bogotá.

García, O. et al (2015). "Artisanal Gold Mining in Antioquia, Colombia: A Successful Case of Mercury Reduction." *Journal of Cleaner Production*, No. 90, vol. 1, pp. 244-252.

Gärtner, Á. (2005). *Los místeres de las minas: crónica de la colonia europea más grande de Colombia en el siglo XIX, surgida alrededor de las minas de Marmato, Supía y Riosucio*. Editorial Universidad de Caldas.

Giraldo, G. ed. (1954). Relaciones de mando en los virreyes de la Nueva Granada. Memorias económicas, Banco de la República, Bogotá.

Gómez, J. (2010). "La Frontino Gold Mines y el verdadero Dorado," *Prensa Rural*, 12 jun.

González, C. (2017). *Brujería, minería tradicional y capitalismo transnacional en los Andes colombianos. El caso del pueblo minero de Marmato-Colombia*. Instituto Colombiano de Antropología e Historia, Bogotá.

Grieco, M. (2014). *Marmato* (documental).

Hoyos, J. J. (2016). *El oro y la sangre*. Sílaba Editores, Medellín.

Isaza, L. (2015). *Monografía de Segovia*. Cooimpresos, Medellín.

Langlois, R. y Pascale M. (2012). *Por todo el oro de Colombia* (documental).

Lasso, R. (2013). *Campo de la minería de oro y habitus productivo en Marmato-Caldas: estrategias de conservación y transformación en tiempos de globalización.* Universidad Nacional de Colombia.

Ley 685. Código de Minas (2001). *Diario Oficial*, No. 44.245. Bogotá.

López, D. (2015). *Precioso robo: violencia, corrupción, incultura y desasosiego en Segovia y Remedios, Antioquia.* Cooimpresos, Medellín.

Marin, T. et al (2016). "Economic Feasibility of Responsible Small-scale Gold Mining," *Journal of Cleaner Production*, No. 129, pgs: 531-536.

Misra, K. (2000). *Understanding Mineral Deposits.* Springer.com.

Múnera, J. M. y G. Reichel-Dolmatoff (1988). *Orfebrería y chamanismo: un estudio iconográfico del Museo del Oro.* Editorial Colina, Medellín.

National Geographic Explorer (2012). *Guerrilla Gold Rush* (documental).

Palacios, M. y F. Safford (2002). *Colombia, país fragmentado, sociedad dividida.* Editorial Norma, Bogotá.

Palacios, J. (1982). "La esclavitud y la sociedad esclavista." *Manual de Historia de Colombia*, vol. 1, Procultura, Bogotá.

Patiño, V. M. (1992). *Historia de la cultura material en la América Equinoccial.* Tomo V: *Tecnología.* Instituto Caro y Cuervo, Bogotá.

Peñas, O. L. (2001). *Goldsmiths from Mompox: Occupational Health and Work. Revista de Salud Pública*, No. 3, vol. 2, pp. 143-153. Universidad Nacional de Colombia.

Plazas, C. (1998). "El saqueo cultural de América Latina," *Boletín Museo del Oro*, Bogotá.

Programa de Naciones Unidas para el Medio Ambiente y Ministerio de Medio Ambiente y Desarrollo Sostenible (2012). *Sinopsis nacional de la minería aurífera artesanal y de pequeña escala.* Paper, Bogotá.

Rincón, M. (2004). *Diagnóstico socioambiental de la pequeña minería de metales preciosos en Colombia.* Unesco (Oficina

Regional de Ciencia para América Latina y el Caribe) y Centro Internacional de Investigaciones para el Desarrollo (Canadá). Montevideo.

Rochlin, J. ed. (2015). *Profits, Security, and Human Rights in Developing Countries: Global Lessons from Canada's Extractive Sector in Colombia.* Routledge Press, Nueva York.

Romero, S. (2011). "In Colombia, New Gold Rush Fuels Old Conflict," The New York Times, 3 mar.

Sáenz, J. y M. Rubiano (2017). "Minería ilegal, ¿con los días contados?," *El Espectador*, 19 jul.

Sandoval, M. (2012). "Habitus productivo y minería: el caso de Marmato, Caldas," *Universitas Humanística*, No. 74, vol. 2, pp. 145-172. Pontificia Universidad Javeriana.

Sin autor (2012). "Informe especial: oro y crimen," *Semana.*

_____ (2017). "Antioquia lucha por frenar la minería ilegal," *El Tiempo*, 6 de agosto.

Sintramienergética (2010). "Gobierno empeñado en vender la Frontino Gold Mines que no le pertenece," *Prensa Rural*, 16 jun.

Studnicki-Gizbert, Daviken (2016). "Canadian Mining in Latin America (1990 to present): A Provisional History." *Canadian Journal of Latin American and Caribbean Studies. Revue canadienne des études latino-américaines et caraïbes*, Vol. 41, Cap. 1.

Suárez, A. (2013). *La minería colonial del siglo XXI: no todo lo que brilla es oro.* Ediciones Aurora, Bogotá.

Taussig, M. (2004). *My Cocaine Museum.* University of Chicago Press.

Tobón, M. (2000). *Estudio de las condiciones físicas, sociales y económicas actuales del centro histórico de Marmato y su relación con el plan de ordenamiento territorial, para la elaboración de un Plan Especial de Protección.* Dirección de Patrimonio, Ministerio de Cultura, Bogotá.

Trujillo, L. F. (2012). "Gran minería: Biografía documentada de un depredador veloz," *Razón Pública*, 11 jun.

Tubb, D. (2014). "Muddy Decisions: Gold in the Chocó, Colombia," *The Extractive Industries and Society Journal*, No. 2, vol. 4, pp. 722-733, Ottawa.

Valencia, L. y Riaño, A. (2017). *Minería en el posconflicto: un asunto de quilates*. Ediciones B, Bogotá.

West, R.C. (1952). "Folk Mining in Colombia," *Economic Geography*, No. 28, vol. 4, Clark University.

_____ (1952). *La minería de aluvión en Colombia durante el periodo colonial*. Traducción de Jorge Orlando Melo, Universidad Nacional de Colombia, 1972.

Zuluaga, Z. D. (1994). *Oro, sociedad y economía: el sistema colonial en la Gobernación de Popayán, 1533-1733*. Banco de la República, Bogotá.

ACKNOWLEDGEMENTS

We want to thank the following people for their collaboration in making *La Batea*.

To Gustavo Mauricio Arenas of Icono Editorial, and to Jason Eskenazi, Peter van Agtmael, Alan Chin and Glenna Gordon of Red Hook Editions, for accompanying us through this process, giving great advice, and publishing the work. Many thanks to Constanza Vieira for her rigorous research and translations. And to Ana Maria Bedoya for her thorough journalistic investigations. We are also very grateful to Alexandra McNichols-Torroledo for her translations, advice and help with research. Victoria Sarria, industrial designer, has been crucial in the protoyping the book and conceiving the design. Tatiana Villamil skillfully managed the project. Don Efraín Gómez Lara of Poder Fotográfico developed the film; scans were done by Fabián Alzate and at the digital lab of the International Center of Photography. Don Guillermo Acevedo applied the gold foil to the cover. Of course, we owe much gratitude to Diego Amaral and his incredible team at Amaral Diseño for bringing it all to fruition. And thank you to John de los Ríos, for the video and moral support.

For helping with the complicated questions of logistics and access, we are grateful to Jenny Carolina González, "el Nene" and his family in El Palo, Medardo Tejada, Dairo Rúa and Victor Meneses in Segovia, Francia Márquez in Yolombó, Carlos Álvarez in Caucasia, and Karim Amar Osorio, Mario

Tangarife, Adriana Palomino, Yamil Amar Cataño, and Rubén Darío Rotavista in Marmato.

Also, Amado Villafaña, Pablo Mora and the Zhigoneshi documentary team of the Sierra Nevada of Santa Marta contributed to this work.

Numerous colleagues, friends and family lent their eyes and ears and to help sequence and choose the images, review the text and think about design, especially: Jean-Christian Bourcart, Claudi Carrera, Sally Chaffee, Laurence Cornet, Fabio Cutica, David Ferry, Eric Ingersoll, Jorge Panchoaga, Adriana Rodriguez, Monica Tejada, Joana Toro, Carlos Villalon, David Wood, and Luca Zanetti. Alvaro Pardo, of Colombia Punto Medio, generously provided information. We are also grateful to the crew of OjoRojo Fábrica Visual for the support, to the collective Paradocs, and to our friends at the Fundación Nuevo Periodismo Iberoamericano and the Consejo de Redacción.

Various colleagues have published excepts and interviews about this work while in progress. Thank you to Natalio Cosoy of the BBC, Santiago Cruz of *El País* de Cali, Juan David Montes Sierra de *Especiales Semana*, Andés Sanín and Elsa Henao of *Los Informantes*, and to David González and Jim Estrin of *The New York Times* Lens Blog.

This work would not have been possible without the generous support of the Magnum Foundation, for which we are especially grateful to Susan Meiselas and Emma Raynes. At

Brandeis University, the Latin American and Latino Studies Program, Mandel Center for the Humanities, and the Program in Creativity, the Arts, and Social Transformation all gave generous support.

Journalistic assignments formed an important part of the investigation and photographic work: thanks to Simon Romero and the *New York Times*, National Geographic Explorer and Ruth Eichhorn, Jürgen Schaefer and Michael Stührenberg of *GEO* magazine.

We are so grateful to our donors on Kickstarter and at the pre-sale of *La Batea* in Bogotá who made the publication possible. Thank you for your support.

And, finally, we are indebted to the generous and courageous people of Caloto, Marmato, Mompox, Segovia, Yolombó, and Zaragoza, from whom we learned so much.

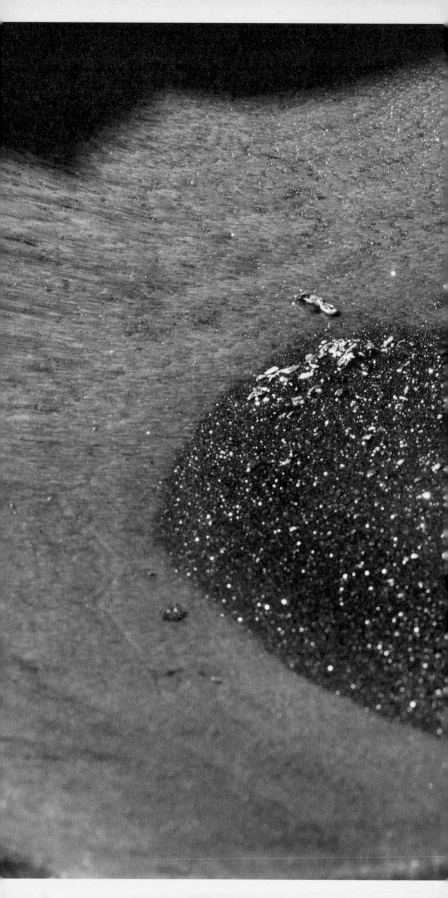

**RED HOOK
EDITIONS**

La batea
© 2017, Elizabeth Ferry, Stephen Ferry.
© 2017, Red Hook Editions
33 Flatbush Avenue, 4th Fl.
Brooklyn, NY 11217
Tel: +1 (917) 309-8866
Email: info@redhookeditions.com
www.redhookeditions.com

Direction
Elizabeth Ferry, Stephen Ferry

Text
Elizabeth Ferry, Stephen Ferry

Photography
Stephen Ferry

Research
Elizabeth Ferry, Stephen Ferry, Ana María Bedoya Builes, Constanza Vieira

Design, editorial and pre-press consultant
Diego Amaral

Initial design
Stephen Ferry, Victoria Sarria

Final editorial design and typography
Amaral Diseño SAS

Cartography
Amaral Diseño SAS / Primary source: www.openstreetmap.org/copyright

Spanish editing and style correction
Gustavo Mauricio García Arenas, Constanza Vieira, Elkin Rivera

Translation
Constanza Vieira, Alexandra McNichols-Torroledo

Project management
Victoria Sarria, Tatiana Villamil

Printer
Panamericana Formas e Impresos S.A.

ISBN: 978-1-941703-04-5

Fist english edition: October, 2017

Spanish edition available

Printed in Colombia